D1261852

"Winfield Bevins calls himself 'an accidental church planter,' but there is no doubt that he is now both an experienced practitioner and a wise reflector of church-planting practice. This book is a gem—concise, digestible, and practical. It is at the top of my church-planting course booklist."

—Ric Thorpe
Bishop of Islington, UK

"Every era in the history of the church has both called for, and given us, the intelligent and anointed young minds required for the day. Winfield Bevins is a classic example. *Plant: A Sower's Guide to Church Planting* has a fresh, yet down-to-earth voice that adds richly to the conversation about church planting in the contemporary world."

—Todd Hunter
Bishop, Churches for the Sake of Others
Author, *Christianity Beyond Belief*

"*Plant* is a beautiful, simple little book for those considering church planting from ground zero and a perfect one for those mentoring new planters as they begin discernment. . . . Winfield Bevins brings all of himself as an inspiring kingdom thinker with connections to virtually every part of the North American church. A unique resource for what may be the most important movement of the church in our day: planting new congregations."

—Graham Singh
Executive Director, Church Planting Canada

"I am thankful to my good friend Winfield Bevins for his passion to equip the next generation of church planters. *Plant: A Sower's Guide to Church Planting* is a must read for those who are exploring the call to church planting!"

—Will Plitt
Executive Director, Christ Together

"This is the book so many in the church have been waiting for. *Plant* is a basic primer on church planting—a church-planting 101 guide—which dispels widespread myths about church planting and sets forth a practical how-to guide for aspiring church planters. This book is not only a gracious invitation, it is also a church planting GPS, which will guide you to become part of the emerging church-planting movement sweeping the world. I heartily recommend it."

—Dr. Timothy C. Tennent
President, Professor of World Christianity
Asbury Theological Seminary

"*Plant* was incredibly encouraging to me because I'm still so new to this idea of church planting. As I read, I felt a great sense of peace that this could be an opportunity to attempt something great for the kingdom of God!"

—Brain Knox
Asbury Seminary Student and Potential Church Planter

"Dr. Bevins has put together something that is greatly needed: a simple and practical guide that does not make church planting the responsibility of ministry professionals alone, but brings it within the reach of the entire global church. He provides a clear pathway . . . with compelling and highly understandable prose, dialogical style, biblical content, and principle-based instruction. Church planting is firmly rooted in the Great Commission and is presented from a movement perspective. Potential church planters, both lay and theologically trained, will find a helpful apologetic to recruit others to this global cause. If you want to see many mobilized and pointed in the right direction, use this book!"

—Dr. Gene Wilson
Church Planting Catalyst and Director, ReachGlobal
Co-Author, *Global Church Planting*

"Start here! Network or denominational leaders should place *Plant* in the hands of as many people as possible. This primer is culture creating and will help individuals catch a vision for what can happen through church planting."

—Jeff Olive
Director of New Church Development,
Texas Annual Conference of the
United Methodist Church
Editor, Seedbed Church Planter Collective

"In a world of scholarly tomes and academic volumes, it is refreshing to read a primer on the subject of church planting. In *Plant: A Sower's Guide to Church Planting*, Dr. Winfield Bevins gives us concise biblical, historical, and field-tested wisdom around the art of planting new faith communities. This book will help awaken church leaders, lay persons, and clergy to the faith-filled possibilities and adventures of church planting."

—Jorge Acevedo
Lead Pastor, Grace Church,
a multi-site United Methodist congregation,
Cape Coral, Fort Myers, and Sarasota, Florida;
Sioux Falls, South Dakota

"As a church planter and coach, I am frequently asked, 'Where do I begin?' Now, I have a great resource. *Plant: A Sower's Guide to Church Planting* captures the seminal thoughts, decisions, and practices that every would-be church planter must wrestle with. If church planting begins with a good foundation, this book is the first brick of that foundation."

—Bryan D. Collier
Founding and Lead Pastor,
The Orchard, Tupelo, MS

PLANT

A SOWER'S GUIDE
TO CHURCH PLANTING

PLANT

WINFIELD
BEVINS

Seedbed

Scripture quotations, unless otherwise indicated, are taken from
the New King James Version®. Copyright © 1982 by Thomas
Nelson, Inc. Used by permission. All rights reserved.

Scripture quotations marked NIV are taken from the Holy Bible, New
International Version®, NIV® Copyright © 1973, 1978, 1984, 2011 by
Biblica, Inc.™ Used by permission. All rights reserved worldwide.

Scripture quotations marked NASB are taken from the New American
Standard Bible®. Copyright © 1960, 1962, 1968, 1971, 1972, 1973,
1975, 1977, 1995 by The Lockman Foundation. Used by permission.

Scripture quotations marked ESV are from The Holy
Bible, English Standard Version®, ESV®, copyright
© 2001 by Crossway Bibles, a division of Good News
Publishers. Used by permission. All rights reserved.

Printed in the United States of America

Cover illustration and design by Nikabrik Design
Page design by PerfecType, Nashville, Tennessee

Bevins, Winfield H.
  Plant : a sower's guide to church planting / Winfield Bevins. – Franklin,
Tennessee : Seedbed Publishing, ©2016.

    xvi, 85 ; 17 cm.

    Includes bibliographical references (pages 81-85).
    ISBN 9781628243048 (paperback : alk. paper)
    ISBN 9781628243055 (Mobi)
    ISBN 9781628243062 (ePub)
    ISBN 9781628243079 (uPDF)

    1. Church development, New. 2. Church growth.
    3. Discipling (Christianity)   I. Title.

BV652.24.B49 2016   283/.76713
2016932682

SEEDBED PUBLISHING
Franklin, Tennessee
Seedbed.com

To Will Plitt
With gratitude
for your partnership
in the gospel (Philippians 1:5)

CONTENTS

ACKNOWLEDGMENTS

I WOULD LIKE to thank several people for helping make this book a reality. First, I am thankful to my wife, Kay, and my three daughters, Elizabeth, Anna Belle, and Caroline, for joining with me in God's mission in church planting and for letting daddy sneak away with his computer long enough to write this book.

I am thankful to Church of the Outer Banks for letting me learn about church planting the hard way: by doing it! I am thankful to my friend Will Plitt, director of Christ Together Southeast for his friendship and partnership in church planting over the years.

I am thankful for my assistant, Ross Jenkins, who helped in so many ways with editing the manuscript. I am thankful for J. D. Walt, Andy Miller, and the team at Seedbed for helping me publish this book. I am thankful for the amazing team at Asbury Seminary, especially Tom Tumblin, Mark Royster,

Greg Okesson, Jay Moon, Bryan Simms, Bill Castillo, and Art McPhee. I am thankful to William and Phyllis Johnson for their commitment to the efforts of global church planting. I am thankful to Asbury's president, Dr. Timothy Tennent, for his bold vision to train eight hundred church planters by 2023. I am honored to join with you all in God's mission through church planting!

Finally, I would like to dedicate this book to countless men and women who are planting new churches around the world. I personally know the unique struggles, challenges, and joys of starting a new church. Church planters, you are my heroes and this book is written for you.

THE SOWER'S CREED

Today, I sow for a Great Awakening.

Today, I stake everything on the promise of the
Word of God.
I depend entirely on the power of the
Holy Spirit.
I have the same mind in me that was in
Christ Jesus.
Because Jesus is good news and Jesus is in me,
I am good news.

Today, I will sow the extravagance of the gospel
everywhere I go and
into everyone I meet.

Today, I will love others as Jesus has loved me.

Today, I will remember that the tiniest seeds
become the tallest trees;
that the seeds sown today
become the shade of tomorrow;
that the faith of right now
becomes the future of the everlasting kingdom.

Today, I sow for a Great Awakening.

—J. D. Walt

PLANT

INTRODUCTION

JOIN THE MOVEMENT

THE FACT THAT you are reading this means you are interested in church planting. However, you may be thinking to yourself, "Who? Me? I couldn't possibly imagine myself ever planting a church." Well, you're not alone.

I myself am what you might call an "accidental church planter." I never planned on planting a church. My dream had always been to be a professor, but God had different plans for my life. In the spring of 2005, my wife and I felt the Lord calling us to start a new church. With nothing but a little faith, we began meeting in a home with only five people. After a few short months, we quickly outgrew the home meeting space and the Lord opened a door for the church to meet at the local YMCA, which allowed us to continue to grow. After moving to the YMCA, the church grew to include people from all ages and backgrounds, many of whom had no church background at all. Over the next few years we witnessed dozens of people come to faith in Jesus Christ.

Soon, we realized that God hadn't just called us to plant one church, but He was calling us to help plant many other churches. Church planters began to come from all over to learn from what we were doing. Over time, God used us to help plant dozens of churches and to train hundreds of church planters across the nation. Little did I know, God was actually calling us to engage in a church-planting movement that spans the entire globe.

I want to invite you to join with me in this church-planting movement that is happening right now all around the world. As we speak, disciples of Christ across geographical boundaries, denominational lines, and cultural divides are multiplying disciples at a furious pace. The growth of global Christianity continues to explode and thousands of church planters have risen to the occasion to meet the demands of this growth. Planters have planted tens of thousands of new congregations in order to provide these new disciples with Christian communities.

This growth cannot be described as an isolated phenomenon. Rather, this is a movement of God. He is raising up a new generation of church planters who have a bold vision and a sincere passion to plant new churches to reach the world for Christ. Some are called to plant churches in cities, some in the suburbs, some in small towns, and others in out-of-the-way villages in remote parts of the world. However, this movement is nowhere close to being completed. As we speak, new churches are needed in every cultural, social, and economic setting. These churches are just waiting to be started by those who dare to step outside of the box and join with God as He enacts His mission in the world.

ONE SIZE DOESN'T FIT ALL

In the same way that the need for new churches is diverse in nature, church plants do not follow a single mold of structure and execution. You will find missional, multi-site, ancient-future, multicultural, urban, and house churches, and these only skim the surface of the spectrum. The reason we see such a variety is because one size does not fit all and one church cannot win all. Enacting the mission of God takes all kinds of churches to reach all kinds of people. It is important to take into consideration the culture, race, and ethnicity of the area in which you plan to plant a church.

As for the personnel involved, once again, no one way is the correct way. For instance, some people choose to plant as a team, while others may choose to plant as a solo church planter. These factors are dictated by the setting of the envisioned church plant. God uses connections and regional factors to help shape a vision for how the church should begin.

As with all churches, plants are simply a part of the larger global church. The global church needs new local churches to reach all types of people for Christ. In essence, the church mimics a mosaic or tapestry that consists of many colors. Each fragment displays a different color, but in unison, these individual pieces portray a beautiful masterpiece. Likewise, today there are many different expressions and types of church plants that are a part of the body of Christ. Some new churches meet in buildings while others meet in homes. Some new churches meet in bowling alleys, funeral homes, YMCAs, schools, and even outdoors under a tree. Some new churches are traditional, some are contemporary, and some are home fellowships. In spite of the diversity, each new congregation of believers gathers as a local expression of being the global church wherever they are.

While church planting may be receiving more publicity now than in years past, it isn't a passing fad. The pages of church history are full of amazing stories of men and women of faith who changed the course of history and influenced the world through church planting. Their stories remind us that the Lord can do extraordinary things through ordinary people who step out in faith to launch Christ-communities. Think about it for a moment. Every church that has ever existed underwent a stage of planting and infancy. Even though it might be hard to imagine, even your grandmother's church began as a plant! As you can see, joining in church planting isn't about beginning a revolution. Rather, it's about joining God's revolution as He brings reconciliation through the body of Christ.

ABOUT THIS BOOK

You may be asking yourself the question, "Why name a book on church planting *A Sower's Guide*?" Quite frankly, I drew this title from one of the most prominent themes in Scripture. The Bible uses various agricultural metaphors to describe spiritual growth such as sowing and reaping (John 4:37; 2 Corinthians 9:6); planting and watering (1 Corinthians 3:6); growing (1 Peter 2:2; 2 Peter 3:18); and bearing fruit (Matthew 7:17–20; John 15:1–16; Galatians 5:22). The process of church planting can draw many valuable lessons from the parable of the seed and the sower in Matthew 13:1–23. I love the way that pastor Larry Osborne sums up the values of this parable when he says, "I realize that most biblical scholars see the soil in this parable as representing the condition of individual hearts—and I agree. But the underlying principles are not only true for individuals; they are also true for the ministry of a local church."[1] In light of these principles, I will share essential seed thoughts for starting a new church. These seed thoughts are meant to be practical and also deeply rooted biblical concepts that are important to understanding the work of starting a new church.

What you hold in your hands is the fruit of more than a decade of church-planting experience and personal research. A few years ago, I began dreaming of writing a short, simple book on church planting that would be highly practical and could be used by a wide range of people. I wanted this book to be a resource for people exploring church planting and also for current church planters and their teams as they prepare for the inception of their church. You now hold in your hands the result of that process. As you peruse these pages, I hope that you will engage simple essentials that you need as you begin to explore the process of planting a new church.

At the conclusion of each chapter, I have included questions to help you think through the ideas of this book and to help you implement them into your own context. This can be used as a discussion guide for individuals, church-planting teams, leadership training, or a small-group resource. Also, at Seedbed.com you can access free online videos that go along with each chapter. The videos will help you implement the ideas in this book and inspire lively dialogue.

Finally, this book is not about a model or program. God does not make robots. He is not a cookie-cutter God. Regardless of whether you are in a city, rural community, or on an island, this book will outline general principles that will help you develop a unique church-planting process that fits your context. As you and your church-planting team set out to plant a church, start with the transforming love of Jesus Christ as your foundation and then let people grow naturally. It's been famously said that every journey begins with the first step. I welcome you to begin the journey of starting a new church wherever you stand today.

CHAPTER 1

WHY START NEW CHURCHES?

MAYBE YOU ARE thinking, "Why do we need to start new churches? Aren't there enough churches already out there?" In this chapter I want to discuss why we need new churches and try to answer some of the major myths about church planting. As we scan the pages of Scripture and also our surrounding world, we see that the world is in desperate need of new churches.

JOINING IN GOD'S MISSION

One of the major reasons for planting new churches finds its foundation in the narrative story of

Scripture. The story of creation portrays the God of Abraham, Isaac, and Jacob as one who pursues reconciliation with His creation, and His chief instrument for conducting His mission of reconciliation is the person of Jesus Christ. As we study the life of Christ, we see that He was from the Father and that He focused on training others to carry out the mission of the Father. In His own words, Jesus proclaims, "As You sent Me into the world, I also have sent them into the world" (John 17:18). Being that Christ is the head of the church and the church is the body of Christ, church planting is our response to the sending commission of Jesus (Matthew 28:19–20).

Many Christians and churches teach and preach that missions are something we support or do, such as sending or supporting missionaries in other countries. This may have been the case twenty to thirty years ago, but in the twenty-first century, the mission field has come to us. We live in a post-Christian world where people simply don't know the gospel anymore. Therefore, we are all called to be missional and share in the mission of God. Ed Stetzer, who is the executive director of LifeWay Research, conveys it this way, "*Missional* means actually *doing* mission right where you are. *Missional* means adopting the *posture of a missionary*, learning and adapting to the culture around you while remaining biblically sound."[1]

The missional heart of God is the basis for the Christian movement. God is a sending God who impels us to join Him in mission. According to missiologist Christopher Wright, "Mission belongs to our God. *Mission is not ours; mission is God's.* . . . It is not so much the case that God has a mission for his church in the world but that God has a church for his mission in the world. Mission was not made for the church; the church was made for mission—God's mission."[2] Thus being missional isn't about creating something from nothing. Rather, it is about joining a mission that has existed from the beginning of time.

TWO BILLION REASONS

While we see that church planting is joining in God's narrative of history, we also know that church planting serves this mission through practical means. Roughly one-third of the people on the planet are still without a local church. The need for planting churches in global urban centers and among unreached peoples is growing daily because more than two billion people who have never heard of Jesus now inhabit our planet. That equals 6,500 unreached people groups who are waiting to hear what God has done for them.[3] Many of these lesser-reached peoples are from restricted-access countries and locations resistant to the Christian message. In order to reach these people, we must provide Christ-communities in which they can interact and grow spiritually as the body of Christ. In the words of John Stott, "We must be global Christians with a global vision because our God is a global God."[4]

Yet as we speak of the global proportions of unreached persons, all we have to do is look in our own territory and we can see the epidemic. For those of us who live in North America and Europe, we see a growing number of people all around us who are radically unchurched or, as Professor Alvin Reid defined, "those who have no clear personal understanding of the message of the gospel, and who have had little or no contact with a Bible-teaching, Christ-honoring church."[5] In the United States alone, there are 180 million who have no connection to a local church, making it the largest mission field in the Western Hemisphere and the third largest mission field on Earth.[6]

With more than 337 languages, the United States has become the most multicultural and multilingual nation on earth. The challenge of reaching these people groups is a result of the growing diaspora of people from other nations who have come to North America. These men and women are often difficult to reach due to various language and ethnic boundaries. As we witness the globalization of North America, the nations on continents such as Africa, Asia, and South America are beginning to send missionaries to re-evangelize the West through church planting! British author Martin Robinson wrote about some of these church planters from developing countries who are now coming to the West.[7] They have come from nations like Brazil, Haiti, Mexico, Nigeria, Dominican Republic, and Ethiopia, to name a few. As we view the very culture that surrounds us, we are instantly confronted with examples of a global issue.

In order to become a global church that engages local cultures, we must have cultural intelligence to understand our context. The changes of the postmodern world are real, but the church has been slow to address them. As a rule, the church has been one of the last institutions to acknowledge and engage contemporary thought and culture, and many churches have chosen to respond to the changes in our culture with apathy and denial. It's no wonder that an estimated three to four thousand churches close every year.

How will we reach these people with the gospel of Christ? Experts agree that culturally relevant church planting is one of the most effective ways to reach unchurched people and make new disciples for Jesus Christ. Professor C. Peter Wagner went as far as to say that planting new churches is *"THE single most effective evangelistic methodology under heaven"*[8] (emphasis mine). Likewise, statistics show that it is much harder for traditional churches to reach the unchurched. Therefore, there is an even greater need to plant churches that reach the unchurched for Jesus Christ.

NINE COMMON MYTHS OF CHURCH PLANTING

Now that we have seen the necessity for church planting, I want to address a few of the denigrations against such a movement. After conducting a series of interviews with a variety of people, I have compiled a list of nine of the most common myths that surround church planting. In an effort to help understand the reality of church planting, I have listed fact-based responses to each of these nine myths.

1. Too many churches already exist.

Reality: As we have already said, there are two billion people who do not know Jesus, and nearly one-third of the people on the planet do not have a local church to attend. The truth is, despite how many churches you see in your community, the vast majority of people around the world are not connected to a local church.

Consider the following statistics in North America alone. According to one of the most recent statistical surveys of the top twenty-five churches, many of the denominations in North America are in decline rather than growing.[9] Eighty to 85 percent of all churches in the United States have either stopped growing or are in decline, and an estimated three to four thousand churches close their doors each year![10] Only 17.5 percent of the population is attending a Christian church on any given weekend and that figure is projected to fall to 14.7 percent by 2020.[11] So how can we combat this drastic decline? The answer is that we need new churches that are planted according to a scriptural model!

2. Planting new churches will hurt existing churches.

Reality: Becoming involved with church planting can actually bring new life and missional vitality to existing churches, pastors, and church members. Church planting isn't just for lone ranger church planters, but works best if it is in concert with existing congregations working together to expand the kingdom of God through starting new churches in a city or region. Churches that engage with church planting can be energized and experience new life as they seek to recover the mission of God in their community or region by engaging in starting new churches. The important thing to take into consideration is communication among local churches and pastors. Often times, church planters don't seek the support of local churches and come across as if they are trying to do their own thing. I would recommend that you avoid this at all cost. Also, if you are a pastor or a member of a local church, I would encourage you to find ways that your church can help be involved in church planting. It might just bring new life to your church!

3. Church planting doesn't really make a difference.

Reality: The number of new churches that are being started around the world is astounding! The growth rate of global Christianity is absolutely amazing as church-planting movements have reached hundreds of millions of people from Africa, Asia, and Latin America in tens of thousands of new congregations that have been planted to keep up with the growth. Consider the following statistics. In the last one hundred years, Christianity grew in Africa from 10 million in 1900 to 360 million in 2000, and the number of new church plants played a huge role in this.[12] Right now in North America, we are seeing nearly four thousand new churches being started.[13] Go church planters!

4. Church planting is too expensive.

Reality: Church planting doesn't have to be expensive, and the congregations can meet in homes, coffeehouses, or other locations that do not require a lot of start-up money. If you are talking about raising money for a full-time salary for multiple staff, buying a building, etc., then you are right. There are only a few who can pull off that type of church planting prior to starting a new church. However, many people are able to start a new church on little to nothing. Church leaders like Neil Cole, who oversees Church Multiplication Associates, advocates an organic approach to church planting that is small and focused primarily on discipleship.[14] These churches are finding unique ways to make disciples that do not require the traditional church buildings and structure.

5. Church planting is only for young people.

Reality: Church planting isn't just for young people with skinny jeans and cool flannel shirts. Nothing could be further from the truth when it comes to church planting! Church planting is one of the most multigenerational ministries that I have witnessed. People who are involved in church plants are from all ages and backgrounds. In fact, when I was working on my doctorate, a fellow student named Bill who was in his seventies had planted a church in a retirement community in Florida that had grown to more than one thousand members. I want to be like that guy when I grow up!

6. Church planting is only for a select few.

Reality: Church planting offers a place for everyone to get involved regardless of age, background, nationality, race, or gender. It takes all kinds of people to be involved with starting new churches. As I mentioned in the introduction, one size doesn't fit all. It will take all kinds of churches and all kinds of people to reach all kinds of people. Men, women, children, families, young, elderly—church planting is for everybody! While everyone is not called to be the lead church planter, I do believe that everybody can be involved in church planting in a variety of ways, which we will discuss later on in this book.

7. Church planting is what missionaries do, over there.

Reality: Church planting is needed in every context, in every part of the world. There are new churches being planted in all parts of the world, including rural, suburban, urban, and even mall churches, to name a few. The mission field has come to you, regardless of where you live. I strongly believe that church planters are modern-day missionaries serving in a variety of new mission contexts. We need churches to be planted in every city, region, and nation to reach the two billion people globally who do not know Jesus Christ. As you look around, begin to think like a missionary and assess the needs of your city. Ask yourself the question, "Where does my community need a new church?"

8. A church planter needs to be an extreme extrovert.

Reality: God uses all kinds of people to plant all kinds of churches. There is a common stereotype that church planters are type A, extroverted, caffeinated, charismatic individuals who can draw a big crowd, but I would strongly challenge that notion. Many of the church planters I have met are not extreme extroverts, but ones who share a common passion to reach beyond themselves to see people come to Christ through planting new churches. While church planting does involve trying new things and being flexible, it does not require that you be an extreme extrovert.

9. Church planting is just for people who are ordained.

Reality: The majority of new churches that are started are led by ordinary men and women who are not ordained, and as we look through history, many of the church-planting revolutions that have taken place began with a strong emphasis on lay leadership. One of the greatest examples of lay-led church planting and multiplication is the Wesleyan movement. As Methodism grew, Wesley saw the need to appoint lay preachers to assist him in preaching the gospel to the masses. This was a bold decision on Wesley's part because it meant breaking from the traditional view that only the ordained clergy could preach the gospel. Some of these lay preachers were full-time ministers, while others ministered in their spare time. Part of Wesley's genius was his ability to select, train, and gather lay leaders around him who became extensions of his own personal vision. The rapid and miraculous growth of Methodism would not have been possible without the endeavors and self-sacrifice of those early Methodist lay leaders. The truth of the 1700s remains the same today: we need both ordained and lay people to plant new churches in the twenty-first century.

SEED THOUGHT

God's movement through history and the two billion souls in need of the gospel impel us to engage in church planting.

DISCUSSION QUESTIONS

1. What are the two major reasons presented in this chapter for starting new churches?
2. Do you agree with the reasons the author mentioned for church planting? Why?
3. Are there additional reasons you think we should plant new churches? If so, take a few minutes to discuss them.
4. Where are some areas of the world or cities that you think need a new church? Discuss where and why.
5. What are some of the reasons that you think it is necessary to plant a new church in your context?

CHAPTER 2

WHAT IS CHURCH PLANTING?

AS WE BEGIN to formulate the vision of a specific church plant, we must establish a definition of what exactly church planting is. In the words of authors Craig Ott and Gene Wilson, "*Church planting is that ministry which through evangelism and discipleship establishes reproducing kingdom communities of believers in Jesus Christ who are committed to fulfilling biblical purposes under local spiritual leaders.*"[1] In other words, it's all about making disciples in every home, every town, every city, and every nation. Church planting is simply a community model of answering the call of Christ to "Go therefore and make disciples" (Matt. 28:19).

Church planting is joining in God's mission to make disciples through starting new kingdom communities of believers in Jesus Christ in every context. Church planting is a natural outgrowth of answering Jesus' call to "come . . . and follow Me" (Mark 8:34; 10:21; Luke 9:23; 18:22) and "go therefore and make disciples." It involves living out the greatest commandments and fulfilling the Great Commission through the starting of new churches in every context. It begins with a holy love for God and manifests itself in the world through a radical love for others.

The work of discipleship is not a program that has a beginning and an ending point. Rather, it is an ongoing process that is dynamic and organic in nature. In the words of Ed Stetzer, "Discipleship is not just a course or series of studies. Discipleship begins with conversion and continues as an ongoing process. 'Make disciples' means that the church is to win people to Christ and grow these new converts in the faith. That process is meant to take place in the local church."[2] Therefore, the call of discipleship is an absolute essential to the work of church planting.

When talking about church planting, it is important to note that we are talking about planting "churches." A church is not a building or a non-profit community organization. The word church comes from the Greek word *ecclessia* which means "called out." The church is a body of believers who have been called out by Jesus to be His body in heaven and on earth. At its most basic level, the church is the body of Jesus Christ. There is only one true church, and it is made up of all true believers in Jesus Christ. The apostle Paul reminds us, "Just as a body, though one, has many parts, but all its many parts form one body, so it is with Christ. . . . Even so the body is not made up of one part but of many" (1 Cor. 12:12–14). Just as the physical body has to have a structure to hold it together while allowing it to grow and develop, the body of Christ has an organic structure where each member has a role to play. If one member of the body is out of place or is not working, the rest of the body suffers as a result (1 Corinthians 12:26).

Today there are many different expressions of the local church, which represent the body of Christ. The church in Africa looks different than the church in Texas; each one is called to be the church in its unique context and culture. One of the best experiences of my life was spending a summer traveling across the countryside of Peru. I was able to visit and worship with dozens of different churches throughout the country—churches in cities, jungles, and the Andes Mountains. Each church was a little different; however, they all had one thing in common: they are all members of the body of Jesus Christ. This experience profoundly shaped my vision of multicultural church planting.

As we progress into defining a church based on its discipleship intentions, I want to dissect what I think is an excellent working definition of church planting provided by Professor Aubrey Malphurs. He wrote, "I define church planting as an exhausting but exciting venture of faith, the planned process of starting and growing local churches based on Jesus' promise to build his church and in obedience to his Great Commission."[3] Based on the pillars of this model, church planting is:

Exhausting

Be forewarned: church planting is not for the faint of heart. It is exhausting and will require a radical commitment to the work. The road to church planting is littered with pastors who have burned out, committed moral failure, or simply walked away from the ministry. For many, what started out as an exciting adventure ended up as a nightmare. Therefore, I encourage everyone who is thinking and praying about church planting to count the cost and to know that it will be hard work. Know that church planting will be challenging to your family, finances, and faith. At the same time, not all church-planting ventures end in disaster, failure, or frustration. Many church planters can and do thrive in various contexts, but it is still important to do your homework and know facts about church planting before you begin.

Venture of Faith

Church planting is not just a good idea; it is a work of faith from beginning to end. Church planting mimics an entrepreneurial endeavor in that it involves starting something from nothing, but the success is rooted in God's grace and in human efforts alone. Planting begins with a seed of faith that must be grown and involves hard work and prayer to do the impossible of starting a new church. We can't build a church on our own strength or merit; it is a work of grace from beginning to end. In the great faith chapter of the Bible, we are told that "without faith it is impossible to please Him, for he who comes to God must believe that He is, and that He is a rewarder of those who diligently seek Him" (Heb. 11:6). The Lord promises to respond to our prayer of faith. If you are considering starting a new church, ask the Lord to give you a bold faith for the work.

Planned Process

While church planting is organic, it will require a lot of planning and preparation. In other words, church planting doesn't just happen; it is a deliberate and intentional planned process. For some reason, certain people think that planning is unspiritual. Nothing could be further from the truth. In the words of Habakkuk, "Write the vision; make it plain on tablets, so he may run who reads it" (Hab. 2:2 ESV). Developing a church-planting plan will help others join in what God is calling you to do. It will let people know the facts about how they can help. I have learned that people want to help if they are properly informed, so communication is the key. You will be amazed how willing people are to join the cause of church planting if they know the "what" and "why." Developing a plan will help you accomplish this goal by empowering the people to achieve the vision God has given you to plant a new church.

Involves Starting and Growing

Church planting involves both starting new churches and growing them. Starting a new church is like having a baby. When the new church plant is like an infant, it will require lots of nurture and care. The work of church planting doesn't stop once a church is planted, but carries on throughout the life of the new church. The evolution of the church involves growing disciples by developing systems and structures for spiritual growth. Just as the physical body must have an organic structure to hold it together while allowing it to grow and develop, likewise the body of Christ must have an organic structure that can do the same. As a new church continues to grow and change, it will outgrow its old systems and structures and so we must adapt. As Leonard Sweet claimed, "We must develop ministries that continually adjust and change with our continually changing culture."[4] In a similar way, a new church's discipleship strategy must be structured enough to maintain order, but organic enough to change with the ongoing needs of the church as it grows or it will hinder its growth. Therefore, the church-planting strategy must be organic and focus on both starting and growing a new church from beginning to end.

Jesus' Promise to Build His Church

Church planting reminds us that Jesus is the author and finisher of our faith and He is the One who builds His church. Jesus told Peter, "I tell you that you are Peter, and on this rock I will build my church, and the gates of Hades will not overcome it" (Matt. 16:18 NIV). Church planting begins and ends with Jesus Christ. The word Christian carries the meaning of being "Christ-like." Therefore, a proper Christology is the place to start if we are really going to plant new churches. I have seen a lot of church planters think that the church belongs to them, but nothing could damage the church more than this belief! Church leaders can use church-growth principles to plant churches, but only Christ can save and grow people into disciples of Jesus Christ. As you seek to plant a new church, don't ever forget that the new church belongs to Jesus Christ and He is the One who will take care of it.

Obedience to the Great Commission

As we discussed in the last chapter, one of the primary reasons for planting new churches is an act of obedience to "go therefore and make disciples of all the nations." When Jesus said, "make disciples," the disciples understood it to mean more than simply getting someone to believe in Jesus; they interpreted it to mean that they should make out of others what Jesus made out of them. Don't ever forget that the goal of church planting is ultimately disciple making. Once you answer the call of God on your life, select a course of action, and then go for it! What do you have to lose? You will never know exactly what God can do until you step out in faith. The old Nike slogan says it all, "Just Do It!" God will lead and guide you as you begin to step out in faith. Beginning a new faith community is the key to reaching your city for Jesus Christ

FRESH EXPRESSIONS OF BEING CHURCH

I would expand the definition of church planting to include many different forms of birthing new faith communities. Fresh Expressions is one of the most effective models with which I have interacted and participated. This movement is a global movement that advocates a "form of church for our changing culture, established primarily for the benefit of people who are not yet members of any church."[5] Within this definition, I want to highlight the importance of the unchurched. The church-planting movement doesn't exist to "steal" members from other churches. Instead, it exists as a tool to reach the lost with the gospel of Christ, and the Fresh Expressions movement has proven itself to be effective at doing just that. While each fresh expression of church is uniquely different depending on the context, they do operate according to a few guiding principles. Fresh expressions are:

* Missional—serving those not currently served by any church;
* Incarnational—listening to people and entering their culture;
* Discipling—helping people enter more fully into the life of Christ;
* Ecclesial—forming church.[6]

While fresh expressions of church may look radically different from more traditional expressions of the church, they are best launched in partnership with an established church. In other words, fresh expressions aren't just isolated ways of being church, but connected with the established churches in a significant way. However, as previously stated, while they are best connected to existing churches, the goal is not to attract people to the existing church. The aim of a fresh expression isn't to provide a steppingstone into an existing church, but to form a new kind of church that steps out in its own right.[7] If you wish to learn more about the Fresh Expressions movement, you can visit their website at http://freshexpressionsus.org.

REPLANTING AN EXISTING CHURCH

Church planting entails creating a new congregation where none existed before, but a close relative of church planting is replanting or re-missioning existing churches. Replanting happens when a church that is in decline or dying decides to face their state and dares to start over again for the sake of advancing the gospel. Graham Singh of National Networks Catalyst of Church Planting Canada called this "dead alive churches."[8]

Replanting requires churches to be willing to create a new identity, empower new leaders, and reach new people for Jesus. Rather than selling their building, in many cases older churches are opening their doors to allow new churches to be planted within their building and thus becoming a midwife for new churches. It may also mean that a church sells their building and puts that money back into church planting. The reality is that very few churches have the honesty and humility to admit that it's over and even less have the courage to do what it takes to replant. As you seek to participate in God's mission, pray and ask God if He may be leading you in the direction of replanting.

Regardless of the approach or model, church planting is one of the greatest ways to make disciples. In the end, starting new churches will require Christians to think outside of the box and to engage their culture with the gospel of Christ in fresh new ways. Theologian Francis Shaeffer reminds us, "Every generation of Christians has this problem of learning how to speak meaningfully to its own age. It cannot be solved without an understanding of the changing existential situation which it faces."[9] We should all share in the responsibility of impacting the nations for Christ through planting new churches, establishing fresh expressions, or replanting existing churches.

SEED THOUGHT

Church planting is a natural outgrowth of answering Jesus' call to "come . . . and follow Me" and "go therefore and make disciples."

DISCUSSION QUESTIONS

1. Based on reading this chapter, what is a working definition of church planting?
2. Do you agree with the author's definition of church planting given in this chapter?
3. Would you define church planting differently?
4. How does church planting involve both evangelism and discipleship?
5. How has this chapter helped to clarify your understanding of what it means to plant a new church?

CHAPTER 3

WHAT DRIVES NEW CHURCHES?

IF YOU WERE to walk to your car right now and open up the hood, you would be confronted with a mass of metal, wiring, plastic, tubes, and valves (unless of course you own a classic VW Bug). For the average person, this jumbled mess represents the driving force of the car: the engine. But to the trained eye, this overwhelming conglomeration of stuff represents intricate relationships that form the whole of the engine. Each part plays a role, and if one part is missing, the engine no longer functions at full capacity or at all! In fact, many of these elements in engines are universal to all brands of engines and they are crucial to its function. In the same way, the whole of a church is formed by numerous pieces that function as one body. While each church may be unique in its own right, all churches share certain pillars that constitute a thriving body.

As I have said throughout the book, it will take all kinds of churches to reach all kinds of people: large churches, small churches, traditional churches, nontraditional churches, churches being planted in schools, prisons, storefronts, coffeehouses, and homes. Although contexts may change, I do believe that there are common biblical patterns or marks that successful new churches possess.

Missiologist Roland Allen believed that the modern church needed to recover the missionary methods of the apostle Paul and the early church for the spontaneous expansion of the gospel. He claimed, "It would be difficult to find any better model than the Apostle in the work of establishing new churches. At any rate this much is certain, that the Apostle's methods succeeded exactly where ours have failed."[1]

With the early church movement in mind, this chapter will explore the essential, replicable elements that are common to church-planting movements. I have primarily drawn these six essentials from the book of Acts, which is a church-planting manual that records the explosive growth of the early church through several key phases. This church-planting movement began in Jerusalem (Acts 1–7), grew to Judea and Samaria (Acts 8–12), and eventually expanded into the world (Acts 13–28). I have also observed these from my personal experience and observations in studying church-planting movements throughout the last ten years.[2] The result is six simple essentials that you will need as you begin planting a new church. As I will show, these essentials are found in the Bible and throughout the pages of church history and in every great Christian movement.

CHRIST-CENTERED

Christ is the foundation and the reason why we plant churches. The foundation of church planting and the entire Christian faith is Jesus Christ, and removing Him as this foundation is the most crippling error any church can commit. Sadly, I have seen people try to plant churches for many different reasons. Some have tried to plant out of pride; some for fame or recognition; and others have tried to plant churches out of strife or envy. These methods lead to disaster because Christ must be the reason for and the foundation of every new church plant. As we review Scripture, we see that Christ is the cornerstone (Ephesians 2:20) and the establisher (Matthew 16:18) of the church. Make sure that your church-planting endeavors are built upon the solid rock of Christ.

On a more personal level, when we look at the pages of church history, we see that every major Christian movement begins with a life-changing encounter with the living Christ. In his book *Movements That Change the World*, Steve Addison purported, "History is made by men and women of faith who have met with the living God."[3] Think about it. Moses met with God in the burning bush. Paul encountered Christ on the road to Damascus. Wesley encountered Christ at Aldersgate. Augustine encountered God under a tree. Luther encountered Christ in the Bible. Saint Francis encountered God at the cross. Saint Patrick encountered God in a dream. Church history is full of stories of individuals who had a life-transforming experience with the risen Christ that left them forever changed. Are we any better or different than these pillars of history? I think not! We must have the same life-changing encounter with Christ that inspired the great heroes of the faith if we are going to plant churches.

Christ, however, isn't just the organizational and personal foundation of the church and its members; He is also the message that is proclaimed. Upon departing for America, Thomas Coke asked John Wesley what message he should proclaim. Wesley responded by saying, "Offer them Christ." As church planters, we have nothing to offer people but Jesus Christ. Our call is to offer them Christ. In the burning words of John Wesley, "You have nothing to do but to save souls. Therefore spend and be spent in this work. And go not only to those that need you, but to those that need you most."[4] When starting a new church, make sure that Christ is the center of everything that you do and everything that you teach.

SPIRIT EMPOWERED

The early church came alive and grew exponentially after the Holy Spirit came upon them on the day of Pentecost (Acts 1:8). Church planting is hard work and you cannot and should not attempt to do it in your own strength or understanding. If we are going to plant churches in the twenty-first century, we need a fresh touch of the power and presence of the Holy Spirit. Without the Holy Spirit, there can be no church because the church is the community of the Spirit. Therefore, without the Holy Spirit there cannot begin any genuine church planting endeavors.

As a church planter, it is vital that you have a personal ongoing experience of the Holy Spirit. Don't be ashamed to ask for the Holy Spirit to give you power to be a witness because it's a biblical promise. In Acts, the church prayed, "grant to Your servants that with all boldness they may speak Your word" and then it says that when they finished praying "they were all filled with the Holy Spirit, and they spoke the word of God with boldness" (Acts 4:29, 31). Ask the Lord for boldness, open your heart, and let the Holy Spirit give you power to do His work. This means that we are to surrender our lives daily and yield ourselves to the Spirit's influence and guidance. Church planting is tough sometimes, and the indwelling of the Spirit is the only power through which God has called us to do work.

LAY DRIVEN

The explosive growth of the early church can be explained in only one way: lay leadership. On the day of Pentecost three thousand were added to the church and they began to meet in home gatherings that were led by lay people. The role of lay people in the life and mission of a new church cannot be overestimated. Regardless of the context, there is nothing more powerful than when ordinary men and women do the effective work of ministry in a new church.

One of the most common features of church-planting movements around the world is lay leadership, not professional clergy. David Garrison, who is a pioneer in the understanding of church planting movements, said, "In church planting movements the laity are clearly in the drivers seat. Unpaid, non-professional common men and women are leading the churches. . . . Lay leadership is firmly grounded in the doctrine of the priesthood of the believer—the most egalitarian doctrine ever set forth."[5]

DISCIPLESHIP ORIENTED

For a new church to be healthy and grow, it must develop an intentional and natural process for making disciples. Disciples are made through building a biblical, Christ-centered community. When reading the book of Acts, we can see that the life of the early church revolved around community. Community is an intimate union in which Christians can share. This is not just friendship, but a deep bond that only Christians can know as the family of God. The Christian life consists of living together in community with one another and Christ.

Practically speaking, small groups are one of the most effective ways that churches have used to make disciples. The Christian life finds its fulfillment when we share it together with one another and in Christ. Small groups provide a place for spiritual growth, intimacy, accountability, and protection. The church is not a building but the family of God and the body of Christ. The people that we connect with in small groups become our spiritual family that support and encourage us. Through true fellowship in small groups, we experience and share the love of God with our brothers and sisters in Christ. These groups become atmospheres where spiritual formation is actualized through fellowship.

MEANS OF GRACE

The church in Acts was committed to regular spiritual practices: "to the apostles' teaching and to the fellowship, to the breaking of bread and to prayer" (Acts 2:42 NIV). John Wesley called these spiritual practices the means of grace. He said, "The chief of these means are prayer, whether in secret or with the great congregation; searching the Scriptures; (which implies reading, hearing, and meditating thereon); and receiving the Lord's supper, eating bread and drinking wine in remembrance of him: And these we believe to be ordained of God, as the ordinary channels of conveying his grace to the souls of men."[6] The means of grace are spiritual practices and ways that God provides spiritual growth for believers. Many of these God-given means have been lost to the church of today and desperately need to be recovered.

We all have rhythms, routines, and rituals that make up our daily lives. We are creatures of habit. Many of us wake up in the morning, drink a cup of coffee, brush our teeth, and read our newspaper. Or maybe we start the day off with a simple prayer and Bible reading. Routines and rituals are not a bad thing. They keep us on track and remind us of what matters most. Spiritual practices are rhythms of grace that help us grow in our daily walk with Christ. Encouraging your church members to embrace and practice the means of grace will help them integrate their faith into their daily lives.

The means of grace are essential to the life and health of all believers and should be taught from the very beginning at a new church. These means include personal and corporate spiritual practices that promote spiritual growth in keeping with Paul's command to "discipline yourself for the purpose of godliness" (1 Tim. 4:7 NASB). The word discipline literally means "exercise," and spiritual disciplines are essentially spiritual exercises. Just as physical exercise promotes strength in the body, the spiritual practices promote godliness and growth in grace. They are vital to the individual and to the community as it seeks to become more like Christ.

MISSIONAL IMPULSE

Lastly, central to the life of the new church in the book of Acts is a missional impulse. To be missional means that we look outwardly by being both evangelistic and socially minded. It means that we care about people's souls and their bodies. It means that because we care about the gospel, we should care about social and environmental issues. Being missional brings all of life together under the banner of the gospel of Jesus Christ. Being missional is God's way of showing the love of His Son Jesus through His church. Christians must strive to always be like Jesus, our perfect example. Jesus said, "the Son of Man did not come to be served, but to serve, and to give His life a ransom for many"

(Mark 10:45). This Scripture beautifully embodies the task of Christian ministry. To be a minister is to be a servant. We are to serve and give our lives for others. Serving is the example that Jesus gave. We should follow it.

Being missional, also involves biblical hospitality. Many contemporary Christians and churches have lost touch with biblical hospitality. It is imperative that we relearn the gift of hospitality, especially in light of its important place in the Scriptures. The word hospitality literally means "love of strangers" and is found several times in the New Testament (Romans 12:13; 1 Timothy 3:2; Titus 1:8; 1 Peter 4:9). Saint Benedict reminds us in his rule, "Let all guests who arrive be received like Christ, for he is going to say, 'I came as a guest, and you received me.'"[7] We are all called to offer the love of Christ to our guests and welcome them in such a way that they would be transformed from strangers into friends. A new church is a wonderful place to recover the lost art of hospitality and sharing God's gifts with the world.

SEED THOUGHT

Although contexts may change, there are universal biblical patterns that successful new churches share.

DISCUSSION QUESTIONS

1. What are some of the common essentials of a new church?
2. Do you agree with the author's premise that while context may change, there are common biblical patterns that new churches share?
3. Are there some common patterns that are missing from this chapter? If so, take a few minutes to discuss them.
4. How and why should Christ be the center of every part of a new church's life?
5. How is discipleship an essential of church planting, no matter what the context?

CHAPTER 4

AM I CALLED TO CHURCH PLANTING?

I BELIEVE THAT everyone can play a part in church planting. From being the planter to partnering with a planter in prayer, I believe everyone should be involved in a church plant in some form or fashion. Perhaps you're asking yourself the question, "How can I be involved in church planting?" or "Am I called to plant a church?" I would like to offer several words of encouragement for those who may be wrestling with answering the call to be a part of the church-planting movement. I have listed three simple ways that everyone can get involved in church planting along with reflective questions that will help you solidify your call from God.

1. Pray for Church Planting

Everyone can and should pray for church planting. Even if you are not called to plant a church, you can pray for the work of those engrossed in the endeavor. By doing this, you will be following the command of Jesus when He proclaimed, "The harvest is plentiful but the workers are few. Ask the Lord of the harvest, therefore, to send out workers into his harvest field" (Matt. 9:37–38 NIV).

As we begin to support church plants, we can pray specifically for cities, communities, and countries that need church planting the most. We especially need to pray for countries with lesser-reached people groups and nations that are closed to the gospel. Are there areas in your city or community that need a church? Pray for the Lord to send someone to plant a church wherever the needs are greatest.

Pray specifically for church planters and their families. Planting a church is hard work and can be a very lonely business. Church planters often experience culture shock, spiritual warfare, and spiritual fatigue. It is hard for a church planter and his or her family to adjust to new culture. When planting a new church, there is also a lack of fellowship and accountability, and you can pray for church planters and encourage them to fight the good fight of faith. These planters have sacrificed everything to plant a new church including finances, job security, friends, and family. They need all the prayers and encouragement they can get.

2. Partner with a Plant

Another way to get involved with church planting is by partnering with a church plant in your area. One of the greatest needs for church planting is gathering a team and inspiring lay involvement. You can serve on a team or offer assistance to a church plant in a number of ways. Do you have gifts of administration, music, technology, or hospitality? Use your gifts and talents by helping be a part of a church plant in your community or city.

Being a part of an existing church does not disqualify you from partnering with a plant. An existing church can collaborate with a new church plant by becoming a mother church that sends out a church planting team to help begin the new work. Christians and churches in a region or community can partner together to plant new churches in their area. You can also help financially support a church planter or plant. Furthermore, if you are working to discern if God has placed a call on your life to plant, serving in a church plant is also a wonderful way to help clarify this call. As you can see, there are many different ways that you can partner with church planting.

3. Plant a Church

The most involved way of joining the church-planting movement is becoming the planter yourself. Is God calling you to be a church planter? This is a hard question that only you can answer for yourself. If you feel that you may be called to church planting, or simply wondering what's next for you, take a few minutes to answer these questions.[1]

TEN QUESTIONS TO ASK YOURSELF

1. Do you like trying new things?

Church planting is essentially an entrepreneurial enterprise, and you may at times have to do things that are not enjoyable. So, if trying new things isn't fun to you, this could be a problem. At the same time, if you like a different challenge twice a week, this could be the place for you! Planting a church means that you will be doing something different almost every single day. You have to be willing to learn and change and grow. At the same time, there are many things that need to be accomplished every single week; the weekends just keep on coming.

2. Are you flexible and adaptable?

Working unexpected jobs, filling unexpected roles, navigating financial challenges, and dealing with difficult people are all parts of this job. If you can roll with that, taking each day for what it is worth, you probably have the best chance of enjoying this challenge. On the other hand, if you're easily stressed when your things don't go according to plan, this might not be a very good fit. With church planting, almost nothing goes according to plan. That's why it's so frustrating and why it's so fun! You have to be ready to adapt in almost every single moment. You might plan for fifty people and have only five, or vice versa. It is vitally important to be able and willing to change and adjust plans when necessary, all while never letting go of the goals you are trying to accomplish.

3. Do you like being with those that don't normally go to church?

The trick is, all the people who go to church in the town you're planting already have a church. So, your best shot is going to be with people who aren't already churchgoers. If that sounds like a good time to you, planting could go very well. There aren't a lot of churches for people that don't want to be a part of a church. Church planting isn't about "shuffling the deck" of churches in a city. It should be about introducing people to God, helping those who want to become followers of Christ, and welcoming them into the family of God.

4. Have you been recognized as a leader by those that you know best?

The best indicator of future leadership is past leadership. Leaders don't suddenly learn how to lead because they have a title or vision. The best way to find out if you're a leader is to look behind you. If people are following you, you're a leader. Now take a closer look. Who's behind you? Do the people that trust you know the real you? This is the kind of leadership it takes to launch a healthy church plant. Also, those who can best exercise authority are those who have learned to operate under authority in a healthy way. Do those whom you currently serve under recognize your leadership gifts and abilities? And are you learning how to serve under their leadership in a healthy way? The answer to these questions can be great insights into your leadership capability.

5. Do you attend and serve in a church?

Church is a lot more complicated than it appears on the surface. Just having some good ideas isn't enough. You need to have your fingers deep into the day-to-day realities of ministering to real people and their needs. The best way to learn how to pastor is to be a part of a local church that you help to grow and thrive. If you can't serve in a church, why would you want to plant a church?

6. Do you daydream about ways that the church could be relevant to culture?

This question really is at the heart of the endeavor of starting new congregations. We want to walk with our Bible in one hand and a newspaper in the other—tuning in to the Holy Spirit and to the local news. If this conversation doesn't really interest you in some way, vision for a new church might be hard to find. Every successful church planter that we've ever known dreams about the kind of church that would connect with those that don't go to church. They can see it, hear it, smell it, and talk about it in a way that others want to be a part of.

7. Are you a risk taker?

Lots of church plants don't make it. And even in the ones that do, launching a congregation involves trying lots and lots of things that don't work. "Throwing spaghetti at the wall to see what sticks" is a reality for people on the front end of this task. Failure is not a possibility; it is a certainty. You have to be willing to fail in order to grow. Church planters take risks that others have only thought about. But these are not meant to be uncalculated risks. A church plant is not just a philosophical idea; real people's lives are at stake. This is risk taking with a perspective toward the glory of God, and aimed at helping others find the life of Christ.

8. Do you have a desire to teach the Bible?

Teaching the Bible is one of the essential job requirements of a church planter. You aren't creating a new story; you are joining an ancient one. If you can't tell the story of God, it's hard to show where you and your church fit in. Preaching and teaching can take on myriad forms and styles—and this is all for the good. You will learn over the years how this works best for you. But if you don't find any passion at all in communicating the Bible, it will be hard to gather people to a community in which you find yourself preaching regularly.

9. If you are married, is your spouse supportive of your ministry dreams?

It is impossible for a task of this magnitude not to have an enormous influence on your family—and probably at some point, it will cost each of you something. If they aren't in full agreement and support, this sacrifice will cause enormous problems in your relationships. They have to believe in your call, and their own. God doesn't call just one person in a marriage to this kind of ministry. Even though you might be the primary leader, your spouse will have to sacrifice for a church to be planted. When God calls a person, He calls the whole family. You will need to agree together that this is what God is calling you to.

10. Do you manage your finances well?

It's not very exciting, but number crunching is a big part of leading a church. If you can't manage your own finances, what makes you think you can manage the finances of a church? Church planters receive offerings—money that people have given in order to honor and worship God. We must be able to manage it in a way that glorifies God. Step one is learning how to manage and be generous with our own personal finances.

SEED THOUGHT

Although everyone is not called to be a church planter, everyone can be involved in church planting in some form or fashion.

DISCUSSION QUESTIONS

1. Do you agree with the statement: "Although everyone is not called to be a church planter, everyone can be involved in church planting in one way or another"?
2. What are some of the ways that everyone can get involved with church planting?
3. Are there some additional ways in which people can be involved in starting a new church that were not mentioned?
4. After reading this chapter and answering the questions, do you think that God may be calling you to plant a new church? Explain.
5. Did you find the "Questions to Ask Yourself" helpful? Explain why or why not.

CHAPTER 5

WHAT IS THE PROCESS OF CHURCH PLANTING?

AS I HAVE said throughout this book, it will take all kinds of churches to reach all kinds of people—large churches, small churches, traditional churches, nontraditional churches, churches being planted in schools, prisons, storefronts, coffeehouses, and homes.

At this point, you may be wondering, "What is the actual process of starting a new church?" While the context of church planting is very different from place to place, there is a general pattern to the process of church planting that is applicable to a variety of different contexts. In this chapter, we will now turn our attention to the actual process of church planting. I would like to offer the following seven steps for planting new churches as a guide for ordinary people who feel called to the extraordinary work of church planting.

SEVEN STEPS TO CHURCH PLANTING

1. Hearing: Discerning God's Call

Church planting begins with a clear sense of hearing God's call. Any other motivation, no matter how good it may be, is not enough. Therefore, it is essential that before anyone begins planting a new church they must hear God's call. In Acts 16:9 (NIV), we are told that "During the night Paul had a vision of a man of Macedonia standing and begging him, 'Come over to Macedonia and help us.'" Immediately afterward, Paul redirected his steps and left to establish the church at Philippi. In the same way, we must also hear God's voice to receive assurance of His calling to church planting.

Here are a couple of thoughts for hearing God's voice. First, pray for God's voice and direction in church planting. He may speak through a still, small voice in your heart in prayer. A lot of people see prayer as a monologue rather than a dialogue. Don't just talk to God, stop and let Him talk to you. Be patient and listen. Second, God speaks through ordinary everyday events and circumstances. Never underestimate small things that happen from day-to-day to confirm His calling because the Lord may be using them to speak to you. Last, God might use somebody else to speak to you, even when you least expect it. Sometimes God may use someone you already know, other times He may use a complete stranger. The Bible is full of stories and examples of how God speaks through others to share His Word. Don't be afraid to ask God for direction in your life. He speaks to those who are willing to ask and listen.

2. Preparing: Developing a Plan

As I mentioned in chapter 2, church planting doesn't just happen; it is the result of a planned process. Therefore, developing a strategic plan is essential to starting a new church. In Luke 14:28–30, we find Jesus speaking about the importance of planning. He says, "Suppose one of you wants to build a tower. Won't you first sit down and estimate the cost to see if you have enough money to complete it? For if you lay the foundation and are not able to finish it, everyone who sees it will ridicule you, saying, 'This person began to build and wasn't able to finish'" (NIV).

Jesus' words are especially applicable to those who feel that God has called them to plant a church. We must count the cost before starting a new church. Many church planters write a church-planting proposal that helps guide the direction of the new work and helps others understand the vision. Such a plan answers questions like, Why start a new church? Who is this church going to reach? What kind of church are we going to plant? How and when will we plant this church? What will make this church different? What is God asking this new church to do? Developing a plan that answers these and other questions will help you accomplish the vision of starting a new church.

3. Praying: Building a Prayer Team

If you are going to be planting a church, you should bathe it in prayer from the very beginning. Start praying now! As you move forward, gather an intercessory prayer team to pray for you, the new church, and the community in which you feel called to plant. According to the dictionary, to *intercede* means simply, "to go or pass between; to act between parties with a view to reconcile those who differ or contend; to interpose; to mediate or make intercession; mediation." Intercession basically means to stand between two extremes. It means earnestly pleading with a person on behalf of another. Intercessory prayer happens when we stand in the gap between God and others. We live in a world that is full of spiritual warfare and God wants us to pray for the salvation and redemption of others. It is not His desire that any should perish but that all would receive eternal life (see 1 Timothy 2:4). Prayer is the foundation of a church, especially a new church.

There are various ways that you can seek to integrate prayer into the life of your church plant. First, make prayer a priority in everything that you do from the beginning. Start with a prayer ministry that can bathe your church plant and the community you serve in prayer. Establish prayer teams to pray confidentially with people. You can also start a prayer chain of people to regularly pray for you, your church, and the needs in your community. Lastly, pray that God will give you the right opportunity and words to say to others as you reach out into the community.

4. Reaching: Building Relationships with the Lost

The ultimate purpose of church planting is to join the mission of God in inviting people to faith in Jesus Christ. New churches should grow as they reach new people with the gospel of Jesus Christ. Sharing our faith is the duty of every believer. The word evangelism comes from the Greek word *evangelion*, which means "gospel" or "good news." We are all called to share the good news of Jesus' love and forgiveness with the world. It is not as important how we share our faith but that we share our faith. There are many different ways that Christians can share their faith with others.

One of the best ways to share the faith with friends and family is by personal evangelism and missional living. Being an authentic Christian day after day is the best way to lead somebody to Jesus Christ. To be a living witness does not remove a Christian's responsibility to share the faith; rather it gives the opportunity. Jesus said in Matthew 5:16 to "let your light shine before men" (NASB). A

Christian's life becomes a light for others to see God. Therefore, believers should show the world that our God is real through actions and deeds.

It is important to say that evangelism and discipleship are not two separate things. Some new churches focus on evangelism at the expense of discipleship by seeking to win converts instead of making disciples. The goal of evangelism is disciple making. The Great Commission in Matthew 28 is to make disciples who will follow Christ rather than simply win converts. The disciples understood the call to make disciples as a call to train others in the same way that Christ had trained them. Robert Coleman explained the Great Commission in the following way:

> The Great Commission is not merely to go the to the ends of the earth preaching the Gospel (Mark 16:15), nor to baptize a lot of converts into the name of the triune God, nor to teach them the precepts of Christ, but to "make disciples"—to build people like themselves who were so constrained by the commission of Christ that they not only follow, but also lead others to follow His way.[1]

5. Growing: Discipling and Maturing

New churches play an important role in our spiritual growth and development as disciples and followers of Jesus Christ. While modern models may tend to value quantity, these churches should not simply be concerned with growing numbers, but with growing members through discipleship. Spiritual growth and discipleship happen in a number of ways through the local church. However, one of the primary ways the church makes disciples is by providing a place for people to hear, learn, and study the Word of God within the context of Christian community under godly leadership.

New churches can become a school of Christ that helps people become disciples and grow in their faith in a variety of ways. New churches can offer training and small groups that help Christians grow and learn to apply the Bible to everyday life. When I was a new believer, my church helped me learn to read my Bible and encouraged me to pray and to share my faith with others. Learning about God's Word within the context of a new church allows people to ask important questions, dialogue, and learn from other believers who have more wisdom and experience.

6. Gathering: Coming Together in Worship

A new church is birthed as people begin to come together to worship, pray, and learn God's Word. In its earliest expression, the church meant a group of individuals who had come together in the name of Jesus Christ. While the original Greek word for church meant "called-out ones," the modern English dictionary describes church as, "a building for public and especially Christian worship."[2] The church is not the building, but the people who come together to worship and serve God. This doesn't have to be in a traditional church building, but can take place in a living room, coffee bar, or school cafeteria.

As Christians, we don't just gather to stay together, but to be prepared to go back out into the world in mission. The worship gathering actually feeds us and prepares us to be missionaries to the world in which God has called us to live. Theologian N. T. Wright described this connection in the following way, "The link between worship and mission is so close that many prefer to speak of them in terms of each other. Glad, rich worship of the God revealed in Jesus invites outsiders to come in, welcomes them, nourishes them, and challenges them."[3] The God we worship when we gather invites others into the worshipping community of the church. Therefore, a new church is a gathering of believers who come together to worship God and then are sent back out into the world on mission to invite others to come and join in worship.

7. Multiplying: Churches Planting Churches

Finally, don't just plant a church, but plant a movement. Begin with a vision to multiply everything including disciples, small groups, and more churches. From the very beginning cast the vision to be a church-planting church that plants more churches. There is no happier time than when a family is getting ready to have a baby. Jesus expected His disciples to multiply and to reproduce His likeness in others. He imparted His message and mission to His disciples so that they would reproduce themselves in others and make disciples of all nations. The Great Commission implies that the followers of Jesus will reproduce themselves and "make disciples." Reproduction is how the Christian movement was born.

Today, what has become a 2.1 billion-member movement started with only twelve disciples. Sadly, many Christians and new churches will never reproduce themselves. The result is that they take their faith and legacy with them to the grave. And nearly 80 percent of all evangelical churches in the United States have either stopped growing or are in decline! What does this mean? Simple: the church in North America is not multiplying. As you consider church planting, why not plant a reproducing, disciple-making church that multiplies itself by planting more churches?

SEED THOUGHT

While the context of church planting is very different from place to place, there is a general pattern to the process of church planting.

DISCUSSION QUESTIONS

1. What is the general process of starting a new church that was discussed in this chapter?
2. How might that be different in your setting or context?
3. What would you add or take away from the list?
4. Why do you think that it is important to develop a plan for starting a new church?
5. Based on this chapter, what are some of the most important things that you think are necessary in preparing to start a new church?

WHY NOT PLANT A CHURCH?

I WANT TO end this book with one final question: Why not plant a church? God is using the most unlikely men and women to plant churches in the most unlikely of ways in the most unlikely of places. Why not you? If, after reading this, you sense God is calling you to plant a church, I would like to offer a few words of encouragement.

1. Take an Assessment

Before setting a plan into action, I would highly recommend taking a church-planting candidate assessment test. This is especially important if you plan to be a full-time paid church planter. These assessments come in a variety of formats and they help provide potential planters with an initial indicator of their readiness to plant a church. By evaluating different characteristics that are important for potential church planters, these tests offer a valuable lens through which you can evaluate yourself. While there are no magical assessments that automatically guarantee that you will succeed as a church planter, a good assessment will help you get a better handle on your potential calling to the ministry church planting.

2. Pursue Training

Another next step to consider is pursuing church-planting training. There are many different ways to be trained for church planting, from informal workshops to graduate degree programs. Institutions like Asbury Seminary are committed to equipping church leaders through innovative training programs that are theologically grounded to help anchor the growth of church-planting endeavors around the world. Whether it be informal or formal, training will function as the foundation of your pursuit of God's calling.

3. Be Faithful Where You Are

Be faithful wherever you are before you step out to plant a church. I have learned over the years that faithfulness results in fruitfulness. When you are faithful over the small things, God will entrust you with greater things. Serve somewhere and under someone else before you try to go out on your own to plant a church. Make the most of every opportunity that God gives you. You never know when you will make a ministry connection or when you will learn a lesson that you can use later. Never pass up a moment to develop a skill or a relationship.

4. Know Your Community

Holistic church planting happens by getting to know the community in which you feel called to start a new church. It begins by recognizing the needs in your community. You will never know what the needs of your community are until you begin to get outside of the four walls of the church and get into the community. It is amazing how little Christians actually interact with non-churchgoers. Matthew 9:35 tells us that when Jesus went out into all the cities and villages, He saw that the multitudes were weary and had compassion on them. As Jesus went into the community, He saw the needs of the people. Likewise, when you get into the community, you will begin to see what the needs of the people are. When you begin to canvass the city and assess these needs, you will see many people with tremendous wounds all around you. As you become an intimate witness to the people around you, make a personal inventory of the needs, and then you will be able to guide your church's mission in a way that meets the needs of your community.

5. Find a Mentor

As you are praying about starting a new church, I would recommend finding a coach and a mentor who can help you discern your calling to church planting. Everybody needs a coach, a mentor, a "Gandalf." Many seasoned church planters love to share their ministry experiences with a church planter who is beginning his or her ministry journey and these people can provide tremendous insight as you undertake your journey.

6. Be Yourself

Don't try to be something or someone that you are not. Some people think that they need to act, dress, or preach a certain way in order to make it in ministry, and this has especially become a problem in parts of the world that have been influenced by Western Christian television. This is a false perception that leads many people down the wrong road. Nobody engages a person who is trying to be somebody or something that they are not. The Lord wants to use your unique gifts, talents, and personality to minister to others, so use your uniqueness to be a vessel for Christ. Since no two people are the same, no two church plants are the same. There is a unique ministry that God has created just for you. Only when you are who God has created you to be can you truly make a difference for Him. I believe that when you are real, others will perceive the genuineness of the call of God on your life and doors of ministry will begin to open. So, be yourself.

7. Step Out in Faith

Last, if you are confident that God has called you to plant a church, then step out in faith. There comes a time in every planter's life where they have to step out in faith. You need to rise above your circumstances and realize that if God has called you to plant a church, then He will provide for you.

Church planting is an apostolic venture of faith. Put your life in His hands and be willing to step out in faith to pursue the call of God on your life. Just like Abraham, you need to step out in faith and go where He has called you to go. If God has really called you to plant a church, He will make a way for you. You can't escape the call of God. Hold on to the call of the Lord and know that He is with you and will never leave you or forsake you.

Remember to always be faithful no matter what you are doing. Take advantage of every opportunity. Seek more experienced church planters who can help give you direction and guidance as you pursue the call of God. Consider the possibilities of seminary training and education. Always be real; never try to be somebody you are not. Finally, dare to step out and let the Lord use you. There is a place for you in this exciting new world of church planting, and God is waiting for you to respond and take your proper place!

NOTES

INTRODUCTION

1. Larry Osborne, *Sticky Church* (Grand Rapids, MI: Zondervan, 2008), 15.

CHAPTER 1

1. Ed Stetzer, *Planting Missional Churches* (Nashville, TN: B & H Academic, 2006), 19.
2. Christopher J. H. Wright, *The Mission of God* (Downers Grove, IL: InterVarsity, 2006), 62.
3. For a more detailed discussion, see Dr. Timothy Tennent's examination of the statistics regarding unreached people groups in *Invitation to World Missions: A Trinitarian Missiology for the Twenty-First Century* (Grand Rapids, MI: Kregal Publications, 2010), 360. Here, he explores resources from three major missionary organizations: International Mission Board (IMB), the Joshua Project, and the World Christian Database.

4. John Stott, *Christian Mission in the Modern World* (Downers Grove, IL: IVP, 1975). http://www.worldevangelicals.org/resources/rfiles/res3_425_link_1342020737.pdf

5. Alvin Reid, *Radically Unchurched: Who They Are & How to Reach Them* (Grand Rapids, MI: Kregel Publications, 2002), 21.

6. George Hunter, *The Recovery of a Contageious Methodist Movement* (Nashville, TN: Abingdon Press, 2011), 28.

7. Martin Robinson, *Planting Mission-Shaped Churches Today* (Oxford, UK: Monarch Books, 2006), 144.

8. C. Peter Wagner, *Church Planting for a Greater Harvest* (Ventura, CA: Regal Books, 1990), 11.

9. The National Council of Churches recently released their annual yearbook of US and Canadian churches. Among the top twenty-five churches, only five reported membership increases; the Southern Baptist Convention (0.22 percent, to 16,306,246 members), the African Methodist Episcopal Zion Church (0.21 percent to 1,443,405 members) the Roman Catholic Church (0.87 percent to 67,515,016 members) and the Assemblies of God (0.19 percent to 2,836,174 members). All other communions in the top twenty-five said they lost members or reported no increases or decreases. National Council of Churches' *2008 Yearbook of American & Canadian Churches.* http://www.ncccusa.org/.

10. Win Arn, cited in Ed Stetzer, *Planting New Churches in a Postmodern Age* (Nashville, TN: B & H Academic, 2003), 10.

11. David T. Olson, *The American Church in Crisis* (Grand Rapids: Zondervan, 2008), 29.

12. Phillip Jenkins, *The Next Christendom: The Coming of Global Christianity* (Oxford, UK: Oxford Press, 2002), 4.

13. Ed Stetzer and Warren Bird, *Viral Churches* (San Francisco, CA: Jossey-Bass, 2010), 1.

14. See Neil Cole's *Organic Church: Growing Faith Where Life Happens* (San Francisco: Jossey-Bass, 2005).

CHAPTER 2

1. Craig Ott and Gene Wilson, *Global Church Planting* (Grand Rapids: Baker, 2011), 8.

2. Ed Stetzer, *Planting New Churches in a Postmodern Age* (Nashville, TN: Broadman & Holman, 2003), 35.

3. Aubrey Malphurs, *Planting Growing Churches for the 21st Century* (Grand Rapids: Baker Books, 1998), 21.

4. Leonard Sweet, *Aqua Church* (Loveland, CO: Group Publishing, 1999), 8.

5. This definition is from the Fresh Expressions UK website: https://www.freshexpressions.org.uk.

6. This is taken from the Fresh Expressions US website: http://freshexpressionsus.org.

7. See http://freshexpressionsus.org/about/ what-is-a-fresh-expression.

8. http://www.grahamsingh.org/news/ dead-alive-church.
9. Francis A. Schaeffer, *Escape from Reason* (Downers Grove, IL: IVP Press, 1968), 11–12.

CHAPTER 3

1. Roland Allen, *Missionary Methods: St. Paul's or Ours?*, American ed. (Grand Rapids, MI: Em. B. Eerdmans, 1962), 147.
2. In particular, I have drawn from the work of Roland Allen's *Spontaneous Expansion of the Church*, David Garrison's *Church Planting Movements*, George G. Hunter's *The Recovery of a Contagious Methodist Movement*, and Steve Addison's *Movements that Change the World.* I have also drawn inspiration and wisdom for twenty-first-century church planting from the insights from the eighteenth-century Wesleyan revival, which I believe offers a model for missional church planting in the twenty-first century.
3. Steve Addison, *Movements That Change the World* (Downers Grove, IL: IVP, 2011), 37.
4. Quoted in John Telford's *The Life of John Wesley* (Hodder & Stoughton, 1886), accessed through the Wesley Center for Applied Theology at Northwest Nazarene University. http://wesley.nnu.edu/john-wesley/the-life-of-john-wesley-by-john-telford/the-life-of-john-wesley-by-john-telford-chapter-14.
5. David Garrison, *Church Planting Movements* (Midlothian, VA: WIG Take Resources), 189.

6. *The Works of John Wesley*, 5:187. See also Andrew C. Thompson, *The Means of Grace: Traditioned Practice in Today's World* (Franklin, TN: Seedbed Publishing, 2015).

7. *The Rule of St. Benedict*, (Collegville, Minnesota: The Liturgical Press, 1982), 73.

CHAPTER 4

1. The following questions have been used by permission from Multiply Vineyard, which is the church-planting arm of the Vineyard Church. You can access these questions and more helpful resources by visiting their website at http://www.vineyardchurchplanting.com/am-i-called-to-be-a-church-planter.

CHAPTER 5

1. Robert E. Coleman, *Master Plan of Evangelism* (Grand Rapids, MI: Fleming H. Revell, 1972), 101.

2. http://www.merriam-webster.com/dictionary/church.

3. Marcus Borg and N. T. Wright, *The Meaning of Jesus: Two Visions* (San Francisco, CA: Harper Collins, 1999), 207.